CHRIST-FOLLOWER

A DOER OF THE WORD WITH PASSION, DEVOTION, CONNECTION, COMMITMENT

Seacoast Church

THOMAS NELSON

Since 1798

NASHVILLE   DALLAS   MEXICO CITY   RIO DE JANEIRO

Published in Nashville, Tennessee, by Thomas Nelson. Thomas Nelson is a registered trademark of Thomas Nelson, Inc.

Thomas Nelson, Inc. titles may be purchased in bulk for educational, business, fund-raising, or sales promotional use. For information, please e-mail SpecialMarkets@ThomasNelson.com.

Christ-Follower: A Doer of the Word with Passion, Devotion, Connection, Commitment

ISBN: 978-1-4185-4611-3

Printed in the United States of America

11 12 13 14 15 QG 5 4 3 2 1

I will show you what he is like who comes to me and hears my words and puts them into practice. He is like a man building a house, who dug down deep and laid the foundation on rock. When a flood came, the torrent struck that house but could not shake it, because it was well built.

—Luke 6:47–48

[**CONTENTS**]

[**INTRODUCTION**]

Nothing is more brutally honest than a mirror. Have you ever looked at your reflection and been surprised at what you saw? For the next six sessions, we will use Jesus' words as a spiritual mirror. Do we reflect the image of Jesus in our actions? In how we spend our time with God? In our interactions with others? Do we reflect God's image that is within each of us?

If you want to know what a follower of Christ really looks like and how you can become one, this guide has been designed as a tool for you to use to discover that. Each of the six sessions of the study goes directly to the words of Jesus in Luke 6, taking you deep by providing

1. tools for personal reflection on the daily devotions
2. discussion questions for small groups, youth groups, and families
3. action steps to help you become doers of the Word, not just hearers of the Word

Let's discover how to live passionate, devoted, connected, and committed lives as followers of Jesus Christ. You will have the opportunity to discover or rediscover intentional personal growth and experience a deeper level of sharing and reflection as you become a fully devoted follower of Christ.

[HOW TO USE THIS GUIDE]

In Luke 6, Jesus speaks to us, his followers, and gives us meaningful and practical lessons on how to live as doers of the Word, not just hearers of the Word. These lessons encapsulate much of what we believe to be the core of Christian living, and they explain in vibrant detail the fundamentals of the Christian faith. In other words, they're a picture of what it looks like to be a Christ-follower.

This guide has been designed to help you strengthen your spiritual walk as you:

- Worship God enthusiastically
- Connect with the church regularly
- Grow in maturity and consistency
- Serve others unselfishly
- Share your faith effectively

To that end, each session contains the following elements:

Personal Discovery

In this study you'll go in depth with Luke 6, with each session focusing on a different topic in the chapter. You'll start off by reading a short introduction to the topic.

Read

This section is designed to help you go into a deeper study time. You will read a selected passage from Luke 6, making notes of what stood out to you in the text. This is a time to go into the Word and prayerfully consider what God is telling you in these verses. Questions will be available to assist you with your observations of the passage. All Scripture passages referenced in this study are from the New International Version (NIV), unless otherwise noted.

Reflect

The reflection questions in each section will challenge you to look deeper into how the topic relates to you. This is a time of learning from God and learning about yourself and others.

Action Steps

This section provides practical suggestions to help you live out the truths you learn in the study.

Group Discussion/Youth Discussion/Family Discussion

Our hope is that you'll come together with other individuals, couples, your family, a small group, or a youth group and experience this journey in community. You'll watch the five-minute DVD introduction at the start of your meeting and then dive into these

questions for discussion. These discussion questions will help you get conversation started as you hash out what it means to be a Christ-follower.

Notes

This is a place for you to record your insights and observations throughout your study. In addition, you might want to purchase a separate notebook or journal for some extended journaling on the topics in this study.

Additional Resources

If you're still thirsty for more teaching, you can visit the *Christ-Follower* Web site at MyChrist-FollowerResources.com. There you'll find resources for further study, sermon notes, and promotional materials for your church to use so that your entire congregation can be aligned in learning these truths together—from your pastoral leadership to your small groups to your youth ministries. There's something for everyone.

Luke 6:1–11

CALM

Then Jesus said to
them, "I ask you,
which is lawful
on the Sabbath: to
do good or to do
evil, to save life
or to destroy it?"

—Luke 6:9

[PERSONAL DISCOVERY]

CONSIDER **By Greg Surratt**

Stress. Are you familiar with the word? What has stressed you out today? Getting to school or work on time? A problem with the house or a new client? Pressure from family or friends to do something you don't have time or resources to do?

We live in a stress-filled society—too many things to do, not enough time to do them. Too many people clamoring for your attention. Kids, parents, friends, and neighbors all want a piece of you. You have birthday parties, sports practice, and retirement parties to attend, and before you realize what's happening, you haven't eaten dinner as a family in over a week and your calendar is packed for the foreseeable future. We are moving faster and faster. We've eliminated the margins in our lives. It's just overwhelming.

When you find yourself stressing out, something is out of balance. Have you ever driven a car that had a tire out of balance? Or had a front end out of alignment? It doesn't work right. When your life isn't working right, oftentimes what has happened is that something has pushed the important things to the margins so that your life is out of balance. We need to understand that life works better when you order it around God, not your BlackBerry.

What if we superimposed our stress-filled lives over God's Word? What do we find in Scripture that can help us to live lives that glorify God?

In his Word, God commanded built-in stress relief every seven days. His first commands to the Jewish people about the Sabbath are found in Exodus 20:8–11:

> Remember the Sabbath day by keeping it holy. Six days you shall labor and do all your work, but the seventh day is a Sabbath to the LORD your God. On it you shall not do any work, neither you, nor your son or daughter, nor your manservant or maidservant, nor your animals, nor the alien within your gates. For in six days the LORD made the heavens and the earth, the sea, and all that is in them, but he rested on the seventh day. Therefore the LORD blessed the Sabbath day and made it holy.

God made us to work. Work is not a part of the curse that was brought upon humanity when Adam and Eve sinned. Adam and Eve worked. They had responsibilities in the garden before the curse. God made *you* to work. When you work hard and work well, you grow both internally and externally. That's a good thing. God says, "Work. Work hard. For six days, knock yourself out. Go for it. But the seventh day is mine. No work. On the seventh day, I don't want you finishing up what you didn't get done on the previous six. I don't want you planning ahead what you're going to do on the next six. It's holy to me. It's a Sabbath Rest."

For the Jewish people, the Sabbath shapes the calendar. The entire week points toward it.

Nan Fink's memoir, *Stranger in the Midst,* is a story of her conversion to Judaism. One of the most notable changes in her daily routine was the addition of Sabbath rest. In the book, she describes the preparations her family made for the Sabbath:

On Friday afternoon, at the very last minute, we'd rush home, stopping at the grocery to pick up supplies. Flying into the kitchen we'd cook ahead for the next twenty-four hours. Soup and salad, baked chicken, yams and applesauce for dinner, and vegetable cholent and lasagna for the next day's lunch. Sometimes I'd think how strange it was to be in such a frenzy to get ready for a day of rest.

Shabbat preparations had their own rhythm, and once the table was set and the house straightened, the pace began to slow. "It's your turn first in the shower," I'd call to Michael. "Okay, but it's getting late," he'd answer, concerned about starting Shabbat at sunset.

In the bathroom I'd linger at the mirror, examining myself, stroking the little lines on my face, taking as much time as I could to settle into a mood of quietness. When I joined Michael and his son for the lighting of the candles, the whole house seemed transformed. Papers and books were neatly piled, flowers stood in a vase on the table, and the golden light of the setting sun filled the room. . . .

Shabbat is like nothing else. Time as we know it does not exist for these twenty-four hours, and the worries of the week soon fall away. A feeling of joy appears. The smallest object, a leaf or a spoon, shimmers in a soft light, and the heart opens up. Shabbat is a meditation of unbelievable beauty.[1]

When God made the law of keeping the Sabbath, it was intended to be a blessing, like Nan describes. Unfortunately, not everyone experienced it that way.

"One Sabbath Jesus was going through the grainfields, and his disciples began to pick some heads of grain, rub them in their hands and eat the kernels" (Luke 6:1). Picture this: It was Sabbath. Jesus kept the Sabbath. He had probably gone to the synagogue earlier that morning with his friends. I envision it as a warm, breezy day, kind of laid-back. They were just chilling. They were talking a walk.

Jesus' disciples were making their way through a grain field. One of them grabbed a little stalk of grain, maybe broke off the end, put the other end in his mouth, rubbed it together, took the hull off, and was snacking on it.

Some of the Pharisees asked, "Why are you doing what is unlawful on the Sabbath?" Here came the Sabbath police—the self-righteous, religious guys. "Caught you! Caught you! You're doing work on the Sabbath."

The Jewish religious leaders had established a kind of policy manual for the Sabbath. The policy manual had thirty-nine rules . . . thirty-nine things you could not do on the Sabbath, all very well defined. One of the rules was that if you were a farmer, you could not harvest grain on the Sabbath. You could not harvest anything on the Sabbath because that would mean you were working. That makes sense, doesn't it?

But the religious people were trying to trip up Jesus. They were keeping rules for the rules' sake and completely missing the blessing behind God's law. How had the Sabbath changed from a stress-relieving, relationship-building mini-holiday to a complicated, rule-keeping drudgery being policed by self-righteous hypocrites? How did it get there? The answer, in short, is religion.

NOTES

Isn't religion a good thing? It depends on how you define it. My definition is this: *Religion is people's attempt to please God by adhering to rules and regulations.* It reduces our relationship with God to rules and regulations. The problem is, you can't have right actions without a right heart. We must be in relationship with God in order to live in obedience toward him. But religion focuses on people's work, not God's sacrifice. Rules and religion without relationship only add stress to our lives, and this is not what God intends for us.

Someone once said that religion is spelled d-o. *Do.* We ask what we have to *do* to come into relationship with God. But Christianity is spelled d-o-n-e. *Done.* It's what Jesus has already done. It's finished. Because Christ has done the work for us already, we have the freedom to rest.

Do you think if you rested, your marriage would be better? If you rested, would you be a better parent? A better employee? It makes sense. The Sabbath is a once-a-week reminder to stop doing and just rest in the fact that God loves you.

[**READ**]

Carefully read through the following passage, making note of each mention of the Sabbath, as well as the major characters in the story. Feel free to underline, circle, and make notes. What, if anything, stands out to you? What questions do you have about this passage?

One Sabbath Jesus was going through the grainfields, and his disciples began to pick some heads of grain, rub them in their hands and eat the kernels. Some of the Pharisees asked, "Why are you doing what is unlawful on the Sabbath?"

Jesus answered them, "Have you never read what David did when he and his companions were hungry? He entered the house of God, and taking the consecrated bread, he ate what is lawful only for priests to eat. And he also gave some to his companions." Then Jesus said to them, "The Son of Man is Lord of the Sabbath."

On another Sabbath he went into the synagogue and was teaching, and a man was there whose right hand was shriveled. The Pharisees and the teachers of the law were looking for a reason to accuse Jesus, so they watched him closely to see if he would heal on the Sabbath. But Jesus knew what they were thinking and said to the man with the shriveled hand, "Get up and stand in front of everyone." So he got up and stood there.

Then Jesus said to them, "I ask you, which is lawful on the Sabbath: to do good or to do evil, to save life or to destroy it?"

He looked around at them all, and then said to the man, "Stretch out your hand." He did so, and his hand was completely restored. But they were furious and began to discuss with one another what they might do to Jesus (Luke 6:1–11).

1. This passage tells two different Sabbath stories. What seems to be the issue to the Pharisees in each instance? To Jesus?

2. In verses 1–5, Jesus answers the Pharisees' objections by referencing a story about David. Read 1 Samuel 21:1–6. What similarities are there between these two situations? What do you think Jesus was trying to teach with this example?

3. In verses 6–11, Jesus responds to the Pharisees' objections with a question, stretching their understanding of good, evil, and the law. Read Galatians 3:19–25. According to Paul, what is the true purpose of the law?

4. Compare the Pharisees' response to Jesus' teaching with the response of the disciples and the man with the shriveled hand. In what or whom does each group put its faith?

5. With all of this in mind, what, then, is the true purpose of the Sabbath? See Mark 2:27–28.

For further study, spend some time reading other examples of what Jesus said and did on the Sabbath. For example, study the stories in Luke 4:31–37 and John 5:1–18. Write down what you have discovered. Concordances and topical Bibles are useful tools for this type of study. Don't have one? Check out www.biblegateway.com or www.lifeway.com/Bible.

[REFLECT]

1. Do you think your faith is characterized more by laws and rules or by relationship? In other words, do you tend to cling to "dos and don'ts" or to the person of Jesus Christ? Why do you think this is?

2. What is your understanding of Sabbath? Do you regularly set aside one day a week to rest? Do you think this is something Christians today should be doing? Why or why not?

3. Jesus showed compassion to the disciples and to the man with the shriveled hand. What basic human needs did he meet in each situation? What needs do you see around you in your relationships and your community? How can you show a similar compassion in these situations?

4. In John 13:34, Jesus says, "A new command I give you: Love one another. As I have loved you, so you must love one another." Think about your small group, your church, and the body of Christ in general. Do you think they are characterized by their love or by the rules of their religion?

[ACTION STEPS]

⮑ Write out a prayer to God, confessing the ways in which you have chosen law over mercy. Ask him to transform your perspective, allowing you to see others as he does.

⮑ Set aside one day this week to practice the Sabbath—resting, spending time with the Lord, and looking for opportunities to do good in his name. Practice turning your attention outward from your own needs to the needs of those around you.

⮑ Spend time prayerfully meditating on the two stories told in Luke 6:1–11. Try to picture yourself within the story—feel the hunger of the disciples, the texture of the grain. See the synagogue, the man with the shriveled hand. Feel the tension, the anger of the Pharisees. Then imagine the mercy and kindness of Jesus entering into these situations. Journal your thoughts in a separate notebook.

⮑ Memorize Micah 6:8 this week.

[GROUP DISCUSSION]

Welcome to your small group study of Luke 6! What better way to enrich your individual learning than by finding yourself in community with others? The essence of a small group is people in relationship with God and with one another—it is being in community. Sharing your stories, prayers, and reflections is an integral part of this study. By participating in your group, you will grow in your relationship with God and with one another. Bring your Bible, this study guide, and your journal (if you're keeping notes in a separate notebook) as you and your group experience this study of Luke together!

ICE BREAKER

What are some "dos and don'ts" you learned when you first became a Christian?

CHRIST-
FOLLOWER

Reflections from the Week

Depending on your group size, break into groups of two or three and share the following:

- Have everyone in the group review his or her notes and observations from personal study time. Share with each other what you have learned from the readings. Are there any questions you would like to discuss with the group?

- What are your expectations for yourself during this study? How would you like to see yourself grow?

- As a group, discuss what steps you can take to challenge one another to use this study in order to be intentional in the area of personal growth.

[WATCH DVD] Session 1

⊃ *Discussion Questions*

1. Do you feel bogged down with rules and regulations in your walk with Christ? What causes that feeling? Do you think it is scripturally founded?

2. What are the dangers of focusing on the rules of religion over our relationship with God? How does it affect the way we see ourselves and the way we interact with others?

3. Does the idea of keeping the Sabbath appeal to you? Why or why not?

4. How would your life be different (in a practical sense) if you made changes in the way you approached the idea of Sabbath and rule-keeping?

For Next Time

Commit to praying for one another in your efforts to become the people God intends you to be.

Close in [PRAYER]

Father, thank you for this time together. I am grateful for how you choose to expose our hearts to your Word. I ask that you do that today in your own way. Go beyond me, God. Where there has been a lot of me, blot that out. Deal with my heart, and give me the grace to stretch out my hands in response to you. In Jesus' name we pray, amen.

[YOUTH DISCUSSION]

Youth group can be a great time to focus on Jesus and what he taught, and this study on Luke 6 is a great place to start. It's Jesus telling us what it means to follow him in our everyday lives. Some of the details are different, because we live in a global community now, where we can communicate instantly with people all over the world. But the ideas are the same—Christ-followers *do* what we hear God tell us.

Talking about this stuff in a small group with friends who are also believers will help you grow in your relationship with God and with one another. So make sure you bring your Bible (if you forget, download a Bible app for your phone), this study guide, and your notes so you can talk intelligently about what you're learning.

THIS SESSION'S [BIG] IDEA

Jesus cares more about you than anything humans can create.

Memory Verse

"Then Jesus said to them, 'I ask you, which is lawful on the Sabbath: to do good or to do evil?'" (Luke 6:9).

[WATCH DVD] Session 1

➲ *Discussion Questions*

1. What is the true meaning of the Sabbath?

2. Why do you believe Jesus decided to break the laws of the Pharisees? Was he breaking the law of God?

3. How do you show that you care more about the legalism of religion or more about your personal relationship with God?

Challenge

Focus on giving one day this week to God. Give him your time, your efforts, your focus, your energy, your love. Spend time with him for at least ten minutes one day this week.

[FAMILY DISCUSSION]

Message: Spend time with God.

[LIFEBOOK] Idea of the Week

Set aside one day each week to rest and worship God (Luke 6:1–11).

Summary

The Pharisees had all kinds of rules for the Sabbath. Jesus knew that following the Pharisees' rules wasn't really what honored God. He reminded the people that taking time to love God with everything they did and said was more important.

[LIFELINE] The Main Point

We should set aside time each week to honor God.

[LIFEVERSE] Memorize This!

"Then Jesus said to them, 'I ask you, which is lawful on the Sabbath: to do good or to do evil?'" (Luke 6:9).

[LIFECHALLENGE]

Talk together as a family.

1. In his Word, God tells us that it's important not only to spend time each day with him, but also to take time each week to honor him. How does your family do that? Can you think of other things you can do in addition to going to church together to honor God even more?

2. Why do you think the Pharisees were so caught up in their rules of what people could and couldn't do on the Sabbath day? Do you think this made God happy? Why or why not?

Action

➲ Write down a family Sabbath plan. Make the point of the day to honor God in everything you say and do.

NOTES

Luke 6:12–16

CHOICES

One of those days
Jesus went out to
a mountainside
to pray, and
spent the night
praying to God.

—Luke 6:12

[**PERSONAL DISCOVERY**]

CONSIDER By Josh Surratt

Have you ever made a decision you later regretted? A couple of years ago, my wife and I were on a date in downtown Charleston when a young, charismatic guy stopped us in the street and asked if we'd like to come to a time-share presentation. We'd get a $200 gift certificate for sitting through it. So we went. We knew, going in, that we were only there for the gift certificate. We had no intention of buying a time-share. But at some point during the presentation, the concept started to sound good to us. We were like, "You know what? We can afford this right now. Let's do it." But the minute they swiped our card and we signed the contract, the excitement of our new vacation rental turned into a sinking feeling that we had just made a really bad decision.

You know that feeling, don't you? We've all done dumb things. Some of the bad choices we make simply embarrass us, and then some bad choices scar us for a lifetime. But every one of us is faced with decisions, big and small, every single day. So how do we make good ones?

In Luke 6, we come to the biggest decision Jesus ever made while he was on earth. He was baptized by John the Baptist, and God's Spirit came upon him. He went to the desert. He withstood temptation. He began to preach in a temple. He began to heal people. He cast out demons. Things were happening. The ministry was growing. People were following Jesus like crazy. He decided he needed to select a handful of people into whom he could pour himself. He would invest his life in these apostles, and they would carry on the message that he brought long after he left. It was a huge decision.

Let's look at the process Jesus went through in making this decision. Hopefully it will help *us* to make decisions that we won't regret.

> One of those days Jesus went out to a mountainside to pray, and spent the night praying to God. When morning came, he called his disciples to him and chose twelve of them, whom he also designated apostles: Simon (whom he named Peter), his brother Andrew, James, John, Philip, Bartholomew, Matthew, Thomas, James son of Alphaeus, Simon who was called the Zealot, Judas son of James, and Judas Iscariot, who became a traitor. (Luke 6:12–16)

When my wife and I made the purchase of the time-share, it sounded wonderful. We could vacation anywhere in the world. We looked at photos of exotic locations. We would be able to take our family and friends for very cheap. But after the purchase, we realized that "anywhere in the world" actually meant Mississippi, Kansas, and Wisconsin. We didn't do our due diligence.

Jesus, on the other hand, had ministered with these guys for quite some time. He had seen them in action. He had seen how they interacted with people. He'd seen how they embraced and loved people as they ministered to them. Jesus didn't just get up one day and decide to randomly select some people to minister with him.

Ephesians 5:17 says, "Don't act thoughtlessly, but understand what the Lord wants you to do" (NLT). If you have a major decision to make this week, take the time to get the facts. Examine the impact this decision will have on your life. You can start by asking these questions:

- How is this decision going to impact me spiritually?

- How is this decision going to impact my family?

- How would the person I want to become handle this decision?

We have to do due diligence and take time to get the facts.

Some issues in our lives are black-and-white because God has already spoken about them in Scripture. We know we shouldn't buy something we can't afford on credit, dress provocatively, or speak abusively to our families. But there are other issues we aren't so clear on, and for those we should go to God in prayer. Scripture tells us that even Jesus went out to the mountains and spent the night in prayer (Luke 6:12).

When we were dating, my wife attended the wedding of a couple who had made the decision not to kiss until they were married. When she told me about the couple's decision, I was adamantly opposed to us doing this. We'd struggled with maintaining purity, although the decision of whether to sleep together wasn't on the table for us—we knew what God had to say about that. As time went on, I felt the urge to pray extensively over whether God was calling us to draw the line at kissing. It was unusual, but through prayer, we ultimately felt it was what God wanted from us as well. This was part of our life that was uncertain, unclear, but through prayer we could see clearly what God wanted us to do to glorify him.

So what does prayer look like? First, when you really want to hear from God, *find a quiet place*. Luke 6:12 says, "Jesus went out to a mountainside to pray." Where is your mountainside? It could be a quiet room in your home. It could be your backyard, or maybe you could take a walk in your neighborhood to pray about some things. We have to find a quiet place.

Next, *prepare for distractions*. When I go away to pray, I find myself incredibly distracted. I start thinking about the phone calls I need to make, the e-mails I need to send, the plans I need to make for this weekend, the things I need to get done for work. All of a sudden, the things I've procrastinated about become very important.

CHRIST-
FOLLOWER

But if you can anticipate these distractions, you can see them for what they really are and ignore them.

You'll want to assume the right position, both physically and emotionally. Some of us may need to bow on our knees in an act of humility before God. Some of us need to stand up and lift our hands toward heaven in prayer. You may open your eyes or you may bow your head and close your eyes, but assume the right position physically. But more important than your physical position is the position of your heart. That might be simply acknowledging the greatness of God, thinking about some of the things he has done.

Then repent. You don't have to scroll through your every past sin, but cleanse your heart by saying, "God, I want to be right with you." That leads us into a position of prayer where we can hear God.

Finally, *allow time to listen to God*. Don't just have one-way conversations with him, where you say what you want to say and then you're out. You need to allow time to listen if you really want to hear what God has to say about the decisions in your life.

Look at Luke 6:13: "When morning came, he called his disciples to him and chose twelve of them." I imagine this was a

really difficult thing for Jesus to do. He had a significant following
of disciples at that point, lots of people who were following him,
listening to his teaching, working with him, doing ministry with
him. Yet he was only choosing twelve. Some feelings were going to
get hurt as a result of this decision. Some people were going to feel
left out and ask, "Why not me?"

Most of the time, the big decisions we have to make have
consequences, but we have to make the choice. So after Jesus had
done his due diligence and consulted with God, he came off the
mountainside and made that decision.

Is there a decision you know you need to make, but you've
been hesitating to do it? Maybe there is a tough conversation you
need to have. It may cost you something, and you don't know if
you're willing to pay the price.

Every choice we make has consequences. I'm living today with
the consequences of buying that time-share. Most of the time, good
choices lead to positive consequences. Most of the time, bad choices
lead to predictable consequences. Are the choices you're making
today leading you down a path that is taking you to the life in
Christ that God has called you to have, or are those choices taking
you down a path that leads to death?

[**READ**]

Carefully read through the following passage, making note of anything that stands out to you.

NOTES

One of those days Jesus went out to a mountainside to pray, and spent the night praying to God. When morning came, he called his disciples to him and chose twelve of them, whom he also designated apostles: Simon (whom he named Peter), his brother Andrew, James, John, Philip, Bartholomew, Matthew, Thomas, James son of Alphaeus, Simon who was called the Zealot, Judas son of James, and Judas Iscariot, who became a traitor (Luke 6:12–16).

1. The twelve apostles were the men chosen to represent Christ. They would be the eyewitnesses to his ministry. Thus, Jesus' choice of men was immensely important. Before every big event in his life, Scripture records that Jesus spent time in prayer. Read through the following verses: Matthew 14:22–32; Luke 9:28–31; Luke 22:39–46.

For each passage, answer the following questions: What event followed Jesus' prayers? What did he receive from God through prayer that he needed in each situation?

.

2. Throughout Scripture, life-changing communion with God often occurs during the night. Read the following verses: Genesis 32:22–30; Luke 2:8–14; Acts 16:22–34. In your opinion, why did each of these events happen at night?

3. Jesus said, "I and the Father are one" (John 10:30). If this is true, why do you think he needed to spend so much time in prayer? (See John 12:47–50.) After a full night of prayer, Jesus chose twelve men to be his apostles.

For further study, learn about each of the men: his occupation, his character, as well as why you think the Lord chose that specific man. What does this tell you about the type of people God uses?

CHOICES

[REFLECT]

1. What is your understanding of prayer? Is it reciting something? Is it talking or asking? Is it listening? How do you think Jesus spent that night in prayer?

2. Have you ever prayed all night? If so, what was the reason? If not, what do you think would lead you to do something like that?

3. Read Philippians 4:4–7. How can we receive the "peace of God, which transcends all understanding"? Have you ever felt this? Describe that moment or situation.

4. If Jesus spent so much time in prayer, why do we think that we can go through so much of our lives without talking to God? What, if anything, keeps you from spending time in prayer?

[ACTION STEPS]

⭕ In his book *Prayer: Finding the Heart's True Home*, Richard J. Foster has written, "If prayer is not a fixed habit with you, instead of starting with twelve hours of prayer-filled dialogue, single out a few moments and put all your energy into them. When you have had enough, tell God simply, 'I must have a rest; I have no strength to be with you all the time.'"[1] This week, commit to taking several moments each day to practice this.

⭕ There are many ways to learn about and grow in prayer. Talk to your small group, read a book, or do a personal study on what the Bible says about prayer.

⭕ This week, give the Lord the opportunity to speak to you. Go somewhere secluded, away from distractions. Spend this time listening for what God may be trying to say to you, particularly if you need guidance in a specific area.

[GROUP DISCUSSION]

Welcome to session two of your small group study of Luke 6!

ICE **BREAKER**

> If you were to look at your
> life as a pie chart, what label
> would be on the biggest
> slice? What percentage of
> time would you say you take
> to pray on a daily basis?

Reflections from the Week

Depending on your group size, break into groups of two or three and share the following:

• Review your notes from your personal study time. What did you learn from the readings? Are there any questions you'd like to discuss with the group?

CHRIST-FOLLOWER

- There are five key areas for spiritual growth—growing, worshiping, connecting, serving, and sharing. If you had a spiritual-health tank, where would your gauge be in each of these five purpose areas? Full, empty, or somewhere in between?

[WATCH DVD] **SESSION 2**

➲ *Discussion Questions*

1. What are some obstacles that keep us from making prayer a priority in our lives?

2. What are the consequences we suffer when we neglect to seek God in prayer on a regular basis?

3. What are the benefits of making prayer a priority?

4. What are some action steps you can take to cultivate a deeper prayer life?

For Next Time

This week, log on to www.mynextsteps.org to take the Spiritual Health Assessment and follow the steps in developing a Spiritual Growth Plan. Be prepared to bring your Spiritual Health Assessment results and Spiritual Growth Plan with you next week.

Close in [PRAYER]

Father, thank you for giving us the freedom to make choices and for Jesus' example of what that decision-making process should look like in our lives. Some of us are making choices that are taking us down a dark road. If we had a picture of where the end might be, it wouldn't be pretty. We want to confess to you that our choices are not honoring you. Let today be the turning point for us to get off the path that leads to darkness and get onto the path that leads to light. Lord, we commit ourselves to you in Jesus' name, amen.

[YOUTH DISCUSSION]

Welcome to your second session of discussion of Luke 6!

THIS SESSION'S [BIG] IDEA

Prayer gives you the wisdom to make good decisions.

Memory Verse

"One of those days Jesus went out to a mountainside to pray, and spent the night praying to God" (Luke 6:12).

[WATCH DVD] SESSION 2

➲ *Discussion Questions*

1. How much time do you spend in prayer seeking God's wisdom on decisions or aspects of your life?

2. How do you think prayer helps you to make smart choices?

3. Is prayer a conversation where you only do the talking? If not, how much time should you spend listening to God?

Challenge

Spend five minutes a day just listening for God to speak. Pray and share your heart with him, and then simply listen to what he has to say.

[FAMILY DISCUSSION]

Message: Make the wise choice.

[LIFEBOOK] Idea of the Week

Jesus chooses his apostles (Luke 6:12–16).

Summary

Jesus knew it was time to choose the twelve men who would be his ministry partners and the ones to tell others about him after he went back to heaven. He knew it was a big decision, so he spent lots of time asking God for help before he chose. Even Jesus needed help making the wise choice!

[LIFELINE] The Main Point

We need God's help in making good decisions.

[LIFEVERSE] Memorize This!

"One of those days Jesus went out to a mountainside to pray, and spent the night praying to God" (Luke 6:12).

[LIFECHALLENGE]

Talk together as a family.

1. Why do you think God wants us to talk to him about our decisions?

2. What's the hardest decision you've ever had to make? Did you ask God for help?

3. Are there things that you'd rather decide all by yourself? What are they, and why do you think we want to do this sometimes?

Action

➲ Start a family prayer journal. Get a notebook and set times for your family to pray together. Write down the things you pray about, and then write down how God answers those prayers. It will be fun to go back and read and give God thanks for all of your family's answered prayers!

NOTES

Luke 6:17–26

BLESSINGS

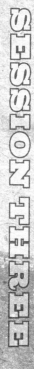

Looking at his
disciples, he
said: "Blessed
are you who are
poor, for yours
is the kingdom
of heaven."

—Luke 6:20

[PERSONAL DISCOVERY]

CONSIDER By Geoff Surratt

Most of us like to know how we're doing, how we measure up to others and in God's eyes. And it's something Jesus addressed when he gave the Beatitudes. Traditionally we've looked at this passage of Scripture as if it's a report card on how we do as Christians. *Do this, and you're blessed.* But maybe we've been looking at it wrong.

In Luke 6:17 we see that people came from as far as eighty miles away, walking for days to hear Jesus speak. Some were sick; others were possessed by evil spirits. Many tried to touch Jesus so they could be healed. The crowds were overwhelming, but Jesus had spent the few days before praying with his Father. His heart was filled with compassion for this motley group of believers. After healing many of them, he decided to speak:

> Then Jesus turned to his disciples and said, "God blesses you who are poor, for the Kingdom of God is yours. God blesses you who are hungry now, for you will be satisfied. God blesses you who weep now, for in due time you will laugh. What blessings await you when people hate you and exclude you and mock you and curse you as evil because you follow the Son of Man. When that happens, be happy! Yes, leap for joy! For a great reward awaits you in heaven. And remember, their ancestors treated the ancient prophets that same way." (Luke 6:20–23 NLT)

Jesus was talking directly to the people who were crowding around him. He looked the widow in the eyes when he said, "God blesses you who weep now." He smiled at the disciples when he said, "What blessings await you when people hate you." This was real life for these people, and Jesus was addressing their immediate needs, not some vague concept they couldn't relate to. They weren't used to this radical perspective. Until this point, they believed that religious people were rewarded with wealth, the spiritual with success. But Jesus was changing the way they looked at life.

It's easy for us to hear these words and think, *Oh, so I need to be poor. I need to mourn.* But listen to what Dallas Willard said in *The Divine Conspiracy:* "The beatitudes in particular are not teachings on *how* to be blessed. They are not instructions to do anything. They do not indicate conditions that are especially pleasing to God or good for human beings. . . . They are explanations and illustrations drawn from the immediate setting of the present availability of the kingdom through a personal relationship to Jesus."[1] These are not commands to be poor, to be hungry, to be sad, to be persecuted. Actually, Jesus is explaining how life really works in the invisible eternal kingdom of God.

The first thing you need to know about the reality of the kingdom of God is that what we see is not all there is to life. We just get locked into what we see, what we touch, what we feel, and think that that is everything. If I can't taste it, touch it, feel it, or experience it . . . it doesn't exist. We don't leave room for a universe beyond what we can sense.

And you know what? If the universe I see, if my experience of life, is all there is, then what Jesus says makes no sense. But Jesus is saying the kingdom of God is more than you see; it's more than you experience. It began before you were born. It will continue long after you die. It is bigger and wider and deeper, and there's much more to life.

Another reality about the kingdom of God is that you do not have to *become* anything to be blessed. Notice Jesus is telling these people they're blessed right where they are. He is not telling them to do anything or to become anything so they can be blessed.

If Jesus were on Earth today, he would look at us and say, "God blesses the drug addict. God blesses the alcoholic. God blesses the prostitute. God blesses the depressed. God blesses the sad. God blesses the reject, the bottom of the barrel, the lonely. God blesses you. God will make you happy." Why? Why could God say that? Why could Jesus say that? Because he knows they will be full. They will be satisfied. They will be healed. They will be forgiven, and they will know God.

Don't miss this. Becoming is a response, not a prerequisite. God isn't waiting for you to get it together. He is ready to bless you today. If we will open the gate to the kingdom of heaven—

the eternal, invisible, incomprehensible kingdom of heaven—by accepting the love God offers, we will be blessed.

What we have to do is just respond to his love, accept his free gift, stop trying to earn it, stop trying to measure up, stop trying to *become*. Because a lot of us are on this treadmill, the treadmill that says, "If I'll just have a longer study time . . . If I'll just pray more . . . If I'll just read more Bible . . . If I'll do all these things, then God will bless me more." Get off the treadmill and experience God's love. Because the truth is, whether you're an addict or a CEO, whether you're a prostitute or a pastor, God loves all of us.

Do not define yourself as *I am poor. I am sad. I am hungry.* That's not the totality of who you are. That may be where you are today, but it's not where God wants to leave you. It may be the reality of what you see, but it's not the reality of God's kingdom. Don't let that define you, because Jesus says you will be happy. You will be blessed. This is a real promise from God. God promises that no matter where you are, he will bless you. He will bring happiness. That's his will for your life.

Jesus said, "I have come that [you] may have life, and have it to the full" (John 10:10). That's the whole point of Christianity. You have to be plugged in to God's eternal life, God's eternal kingdom, to know what full life even means. There is more to life than what you see. What you see today is not what you'll see tomorrow. God loves you, and he wants to bless you. That's the reality of the kingdom.

[READ]

Carefully read through the following passage. Underline those whom Jesus calls blessed, and circle those upon whom Jesus pronounces woes. What stands out to you?

He went down with them and stood on a level place. A large crowd of his disciples was there and a great number of people from all over Judea, from Jerusalem, and from the coast of Tyre and Sidon, who had come to hear him and to be healed of their diseases. Those troubled by evil spirits were cured, and the people all tried to touch him, because power was coming from him and healing them all.

    Looking at his disciples, he said: "Blessed are you who are poor, for yours is the kingdom of God. Blessed are you who hunger now, for you will be satisfied. Blessed are you who weep now, for you will laugh. Blessed are you when men hate you, when they exclude you and insult you and reject your name as evil, because of the Son of Man.

    "Rejoice in that day and leap for joy, because great is your reward in heaven. For that is how their fathers treated the prophets.

    "But woe to you who are rich, for you have already received your comfort. Woe to you who are well fed now, for you will go hungry. Woe to

NOTES

you who laugh now, for you will mourn and weep. Woe to you when all men speak well of you, for that is how their fathers treated the false prophets"
(Luke 6:17–26).

1. The following verses use the same Greek word for "blessed" that Jesus used in Luke 6. The Greek word that we translate "blessed" is *makariŏs,* which can mean "fortunate" or "happy." Read each of the following verses: John 20:29; Acts 20:35; Romans 4:7–8; James 1:12. List what or who is called blessed in each one. What does this tell you about God's definition of blessing or happiness?

2. Notice that when Jesus begins his sermon in verse 20, he is addressing his disciples, those who have chosen to give up everything to follow him. In this passage, Jesus is telling them what the life of a Christ-follower looks like. With this in mind, compare what Jesus calls *blessings* to what he calls *woes.* How do you explain them?

3. Jesus pronounces "woe" to those who appear to have the "good life"—fullness, laughter, prosperity, and popularity. Why do you think this is?

CHRIST-FOLLOWER

[REFLECT]

1. How do you define *blessing*? In what ways do we use the word *bless* in everyday language?

2. Why does Jesus say in Luke 6 that "blessing" is attached to what we would consider to be bad things or to circumstances that we normally avoid?

3. It is easy to say that our reward will come "someday in heaven." But here Jesus says, "Blessed *are* . . . ," a present-tense verb. He is saying that despite our circumstances, we are blessed. Considering your own present circumstances, do you believe you are blessed? What would it take for you to feel this way if you don't already?

4. Much of Jesus' teaching contrasts earthly comfort with spiritual relationship. Make a list of things you desire from life—what you strive and wish for. Be honest. How do these things line up with Jesus' definitions of blessings and woes?

5. Jesus' disciples were willing to give up everything to follow him. They were willing to give up material comforts, to be hungry, and even to die for him, not because of what they would receive, but because they knew him to be life and truth. Nothing else compared. What would you be willing to give up to follow Christ?

[ACTION STEPS]

➲ Spend some time in prayer confessing the ways in which you have sought what God can give you instead of seeking God himself.

➲ To follow Jesus regardless of our circumstances, we must really know him. Spend a month prayerfully reading through all four gospels. Try reading one gospel a week, a few chapters a day. Too much? Try reading one gospel a month.

[**GROUP DISCUSSION**]

Welcome to session three of your small group study of Luke 6!

 **BREAKER**

> Imagine yourself as one of
> the disciples listening to Jesus'
> teaching in this session's passage.
> How do you think you would
> have felt? Would his words have
> been pleasant or difficult for you
> to hear?

Reflections from the Week

Depending on your group size, break into groups of two or three and share the following:

• Review your notes from your personal study time. What did you learn? Are there any questions you have for the group?

• What stood out to you on the Spiritual Health Assessment and Spiritual Health Plan that you created on www.mynextsteps.org? Were you able to find an accountability partner?

• As a group, have each group member share the one purpose area that he or she has identified for personal growth.

[WATCH DVD] **SESSION 3**

➲ *Discussion Questions*

1. Read Luke 6:20–26. What would it look like to live out these principles in our culture today?

2. Do you know any believers who are being treated like a prophet, based on the description in verses 22–23? If so, describe them.

3. Have you ever had to suffer for the cause of Christ? Explain.

4. Is something holding you back from following Jesus wholeheartedly? What would it take for you to give that up?

For Next Time

If you have identified your accountability partner, be sure to meet with him or her and share your Spiritual Growth Plan that you created on www.mynextsteps.org. If you do not have someone in your life who holds you accountable, pray together as a group that God will bring such a person into your life. Actively seek out a trustworthy person, whether a friend, family member, small group member, or church mentor.

Close in [PRAYER]

Jesus, thank you that you love us. In all of the theology we try to figure out, the bottom line is love, because that's why you died on a cross. Lord, help us experience today what it's like to be blessed by a God who loves us unconditionally. As we experience that love, may we become who you created us to be.

[**YOUTH DISCUSSION**]

Welcome to your third session of discussion of Luke 6!

THIS SESSION'S [BIG] IDEA

God blesses his children, even during hard times.

Memory Verse

"It's trouble ahead if you're satisfied with yourself. Your self will not satisfy you for long" (Luke 6:25 MSG).

 [WATCH DVD] SESSION 3

➲ *Discussion Questions*

1. What is your definition of a *blessing*?

2. Jesus seems to have a much different definition of *blessing* than the one we hear from our culture. Why do you think we will be blessed, according to his definition?

3. Have you ever been insulted because you are a Christian? What does Jesus tell us to do when this happens?

4. Why do you think Jesus spoke these words to the specific people listening to him?

Challenge

Give up one thing this week in order to help you grow closer to God. This is referred to as *fasting*. Many people fast because when we sacrifice something that our body wants, we rely on God a whole lot more. You could give up certain types of food, video games, texting, or the computer. When you get the urge to enjoy something that you are fasting from, you should pray to God and thank him that he is the ultimate provider. It's important to remember, though, that we cannot earn God's love—his love for us is constant no matter what we do. Spiritual disciplines, like fasting, are important exercises in focusing on God, but they do not earn our salvation. Our salvation was earned by God's sacrifice for us—Christ's death on the cross.

[FAMILY DISCUSSION]

Message: God blesses those who follow him.

[LIFEBOOK] Idea of the Week

Jesus teaches about blessings (Luke 6:17–26).

Summary

Jesus knew that life wouldn't always be easy. He taught his disciples that when you follow God, it doesn't mean that everyone will like you and that you'll have everything you want. He also taught them that God brings his people blessings (happiness) even during difficult and sad times.

[LIFELINE] The Main Point

God can make us happy even during sad times.

[LIFEVERSE] Memorize This!

"You're blessed when the tears flow freely. Joy comes with the morning" (Luke 6:21 MSG).

[**LIFECHALLENGE**]

Talk together as a family.

1. Are there things that are hard about living for God? Have you ever been made fun of for believing in God? How did it make you feel?

2. Have there been times when you've been sad and God brought you joy? How?

3. Do you think God understands when we feel sad? Why or why not?

Action

⭢ Make a family "blessings list." Write down all the things God has done for you and your family. Put the list on the refrigerator as a reminder to thank him for these blessings.

NOTES

Luke 6:27–36

LOVE

SESSION FOUR

But I tell you who
hear me: Love your
enemies, do good to
those who hate you.

—Luke 6:27

[PERSONAL DISCOVERY]

CONSIDER **By Greg Surratt**

Is there a person in your life who doesn't like you? Maybe she's spread a rumor about you at school or complained to your boss about you. Or maybe there's someone you don't like, and you know some dirt on him. He's continuously giving you a hard time, and you have the opportunity to reveal the truth about him. What do you do?

Jesus told us the answer in Luke 6:27–28: "But I tell you who hear me: Love your enemies, do good to those who hate you, bless those who curse you, pray for those who mistreat you." This goes against our natural reaction, doesn't it? Our immediate instinct is to fight back; we call it self-preservation. But Jesus was emphatic that we show our enemies *love*.

At the time, the Jews' homeland was being occupied by the Roman army. The Romans were cruel and took advantage of the Jewish people. The Jews were tired of it. And they were looking forward to a Messiah, to someone who would come and deliver them from their affliction, from their domination by the Roman authorities. Jesus seemed as if he was going to be the one ... until he delivered this radical message: *Love your enemies.*

Enemy is a strong word, and you may not think you have any, but you do. We all do. Enemies are people who hurt us, threaten us, or annoy us. A person who has hurt you physically and intentionally would easily be classified as your enemy—as well as terrorists, abusers, muggers, and so on. But what about someone who can hurt you financially or emotionally? Do you have a business rival who threatens to claim your share of the marketplace? Secretly you're hoping his or her business fails and you succeed. What about the guy who parks where he's not supposed to at the office? The one who has the frustrating personality traits that you just can't stand—so you walk away? You go out of your way to avoid interacting with this person. But Jesus is calling you to love him.

We're quick to attack, to avoid, and to resent the enemies in our lives. But Jesus calls us to love them. He says, "Here is what you do: When you have enemies who are hurtful to you, or who are threatening you, or just annoying you, you need to love them . . . *love them*." Most of the time it doesn't seem as if it's in our power to do that. And the truth is, it isn't! Only through God can we love our enemies, and he shows us how in his Word.

Loving your enemies means acting in their best interest. And in this passage, Jesus gives us four specific ways to do that.

1. *Love with your actions.* "Do good to those who hate you" (Luke 6:27). Jesus asks us to *do good.* Not to feel it, but to do it. Think of a practical action that will do good for your enemies, and then do it. Stay late at work to help them finish collating their press kits. Mow their lawns. Cook dinner for them. Babysit their children. Practical and good, that's what Jesus asks.

2. *Love with your words.* "Bless those who curse you, pray for those who mistreat you" (Luke 6:28). It's not enough to simply not retaliate; God asks us to pray blessings for our enemies. Say positive things about them, and pray for your enemies. The only way we can do this is through God's Spirit inside us. When someone is talking about one of your enemies, don't bring to light the "facts" you know about how terrible she is; instead, say something—anything—good about the person. Speak for her best interest.

3. *Love with your response.* "If someone strikes you on one cheek, turn to him the other also" (Luke 6:29). This is a call to respond with your enemy's best interest in mind. It is not an open invitation to become a doormat, to enable an abuser to continue in a path of sin. But you don't have a right to disrespect anyone . . . even an enemy. There are some people you may need to love and respect from a distance, but you love and respect them nonetheless.

4. *Love with your resources.* "If someone takes your cloak, do not stop him from taking your tunic" (Luke 6:29). Even those who try to steal from us, even those who would take advantage of us financially, we are to figure out what is in their best interests and respond to them that way.

Here is the truth: You can choose not to do any of this. You don't have to love your enemies by acting in their best interests, by speaking in their best interests, by responding in their best interests, or by resourcing them in their best interests. You don't have to do any of that. But here is what will happen if you don't: Your enemy will continue to be your enemy. Tension, bitterness, and hostility will continue to escalate. They always do. But Jesus gives us two reasons to act in faith and love our enemies.

First, when you love your enemies, *you will be rewarded.* A day is coming, the Bible says, when there is going to be a reward ceremony. It's going to be at the end of this life and the beginning of forever. Understand this . . . it's not about doing all this stuff so God will love you more. God loves you because he has decided to, and you decide to respond to his love by doing what he says.

Second, by loving your enemies, *you demonstrate what God is like.* Many times, as we get to know our enemies, we'll discover there's a reason for the way they act. Perhaps they've been wronged, or maybe they don't know who God really is. Through your actions based on God's love, they'll see the Father. If God commands you to do something, it is always redemptive. He has a redemptive plan. Sometimes our suffering serves a higher purpose. Trust him in that, and love your enemies.

[**READ**]

Carefully read through the following passage. As you read, circle the action words in Jesus' commands to his disciples. Often when we read these verses, they seem weak or timid. A deeper look will reveal that these commands are actually strong and bold and courageous! Which words or phrases stand out to you in this section? Why?

"But I tell you who hear me: Love your enemies, do good to those who hate you, bless those who curse you, pray for those who mistreat you. If someone strikes you on one cheek, turn to him the other also. If someone takes your cloak, do not stop him from taking your tunic. Give to everyone who asks you, and if anyone takes what belongs to you, do not demand it back. Do to others as you would have them do to you.

"If you love those who love you, what credit is that to you? Even 'sinners' love those who love them. And if you do good to those who are good to you, what credit is that to you? Even 'sinners' do that. And if you lend to those from whom you expect repayment, what credit is that to you? Even 'sinners' lend to 'sinners,' expecting to be repaid in full. But love

NOTES

your enemies, do good to them, and lend to them without expecting to get anything back. Then your reward will be great, and you will be sons of the Most High, because he is kind to the ungrateful and wicked. Be merciful, just as your Father is merciful" (Luke 6:27–36).

1. Throughout this sermon, Jesus is teaching his disciples what it means to live worthy of the kingdom of God. According to Jesus in this passage, what are the characteristics of someone fit to be called a kingdom-dweller, fit to be called a child of the Most High?

2. How does this type of behavior compare to that of the "sinners" Jesus talks about? Remember, he is addressing his disciples here. What is he trying to teach them about the life of a Christ-follower?

3. Look back at verses 35–36. The same word translated in verse 35 as "reward" is sometimes translated as "wages." In fact, *The Strongest NIV Exhaustive Concordance* defines the word as "pay for service, good or bad."[1] What does this tell you about our reward? What is our motivation for living this type of life? (See verse 36.)

[**REFLECT**]

1. Do you have any enemies? What about them makes you consider them enemies? What effect do they have on you? How do you treat them?

2. Are you anyone's enemy? What effect do you have on that individual? How does he or she treat you?

3. What role does forgiveness play in our everyday relationships? Read 2 Corinthians 5:11–21. What does it mean to you to live out a "ministry of reconciliation"?

4. Oftentimes the things we say and the way we act are based on how others treat us—we are defensive rather than proactive. Jesus says we are to be the opposite; we are to love and bless and give no matter what has been done to us and no matter how others respond. Why is this hard to do?

5. The Greek word Jesus uses for "love" in Luke 6:27 is *agape*. The same word used in this passage to describe the way that we are to love our enemies is also used in Matthew 22:37–40 to describe how we are to love the Lord and our neighbors. How would you describe the way we love the Lord? How can you apply this type of love to your enemies?

Theologian G. B. Caird gives this definition of *agape* love: "*Agape* is a gracious, determined, and active interest in the true welfare of others, which is not deterred even by hatred, cursing, and abuse, not limited by calculation of deserts or results, based solely on the nature of God."[2]

[**ACTION STEPS**]

➲ Is there anyone with whom you need to reconcile? Don't hesitate—forgive and ask for forgiveness.

➲ Begin practicing proactive love. Seek out ways to bless and do good to others, regardless of how they treat you. Be prepared to share your efforts and the outcome with your small group.

➲ Write out a prayer to God, confessing and asking forgiveness for the times you have responded more like a "sinner" toward others than someone modeling the behavior of Christ. Ask him to give you the strength to change and to begin showing this radical love.

[GROUP DISCUSSION]

Welcome to session four of your small group study of Luke 6!

ICE BREAKER

> When there is a "difficult"
> person in your life, how
> do you tend to handle that
> relationship?

Reflections from the Week

Depending on your group size, break into groups of two or three and share the following:

- Have all in the group review their notes and observations from their personal study time. Share with one another what you have learned from the readings. Are there any questions you would like to discuss with the group?

- Share with the group what you think your top three spiritual gifts and talents are. Do you think that you are using your gifts regularly or not at all?

[WATCH DVD] **SESSION 4**

➲ *Discussion Questions*

1. Read Luke 6:27–31. Out of the several examples of loving others that Jesus mentions, which one strikes you as the most challenging (such as blessing those who curse you, praying for enemies, allowing someone to take something from you, etc.)?

2. Is there a situation in your life right now where you could apply Jesus' teaching about loving others?

3. What are some practical ways you can love the "difficult" people in your life this week?

4. Think about the people who may find it difficult to love you. What can you do to be more lovable to them?

For Next Time

This week, log on to www.eleventalents.com. Once you have completed the spiritual gifts test (click on the "Adult Test" or "Youth Test" tab), record your top three gifts below, and bring your results to your small group next week.

My top three gifts:

Close in [**PRAYER**]

Father, thank you for your Word. Thank you for truth even when truth is hard. Show us all how to apply your Word for your glory and for your honor. In Jesus' name we pray, amen.

[**YOUTH DISCUSSION**]

Welcome to your fourth session of discussion of Luke 6!

THIS SESSION'S [BIG] IDEA

Love is always the answer.

Memory Verse

"I tell you, love your enemies. Help and give without expecting a return. You'll never—I promise—regret it" (Luke 6:35 MSG).

[WATCH DVD] SESSION 4

➔ *Discussion Questions*

1. What does Jesus mean when he says, "Love your enemies"?

2. Has someone ever betrayed you or picked on you or just gotten on your nerves? What does Jesus say to do when this happens?

3. Does this teaching by Jesus go along with what the world teaches? What are the differences? Are there any similarities?

4. Do you have someone in your life right now who could be considered an "enemy"? What can you do for that person this week?

Challenge

"Ask yourself what you want people to do for you; then grab the initiative and do it for them!" (Luke 6:31 MSG).

[**FAMILY** **DISCUSSION**]

Message: Love others as you love yourself.

[LIFEBOOK] **Idea of the Week**

Jesus teaches us how to treat others (Luke 6:27–36).

Summary

Jesus knew one of the hardest things for us to do would be to show love to people who are mean to us. He reminded us that when we love others, God sees and promises to reward us.

[LIFELINE] **The Main Point**

I should love others as God loves me.

[LIFEVERSE] **Memorize This!**

"I tell you, love your enemies. Help and give without expecting a return. You'll never—I promise—regret it" (Luke 6:35 MSG).

[LIFECHALLENGE]

Talk together as a family.

1. Do you think Jesus ever had a hard time being nice to people who were mean to him? Why or why not?

2. Do you think God understands when loving our enemies is hard for us? How can he help us?

Action

➲ Discuss why it's difficult for you to be nice to certain people. Then pray together as a family and ask God for ways to show these people how much he loves them through your words and actions.

NOTES

Luke 6:37–42

JUDGMENT

Do not judge,
and you will not
be judged. Do
not condemn,
and you will not
be condemned.
Forgive, and you
will be forgiven.

—Luke 6:37

[**PERSONAL**
DISCOVERY]

CONSIDER By Josh Surratt

A friend of mine has an autoimmune disorder. She told me that the body has antibodies, which are good things; they fight off disease in the body. But when you have an autoimmune disease, the antibodies get confused and start attacking the good cells in your body and they eventually destroy the body. As I was thinking about it, I realized that, according to the Bible, all of us have an autoimmune disease, spiritually, as a result of the fall of humankind. Jesus talks about it in the passage we're studying this session, and he calls it a judgmental spirit or a critical spirit.

Let's look at what Jesus was talking about when he said, "Do not judge" (Luke 6:37). At first glance, you might think, *I should never judge anything.* But when reading Scripture, you have to take into account the full Bible. And there are definitely parts in the Bible that encourage us to judge in some areas.

In Greek culture, civil court cases were settled in the center of the marketplace because the Greeks loved to watch a good fight. Kind of like *Divorce Court.* And what happened was that Christians started fighting one another in these public places and settling lawsuits there. In 1 Corinthians 6:3–6, Paul was looking at this, saying, in effect, "Guys, this is an embarrassment to our faith. What are we communicating to those who are not a part of our faith when we can't even resolve minor disputes among ourselves?" So, he says, when there is a disagreement between two Christ-followers, we are to bring it to the church and judge it there.

Likewise, in 1 Corinthians 5, Paul teaches the church to judge members who are living in unrepentant sin. He isn't just talking about a guest who's checking things out. This also isn't somebody who's struggling with an issue and trying to find accountability. This is a person who has totally accepted this sin, and the church has accepted it as well. Paul says stop gossiping about it; stop bringing it up as a prayer request in your small group. Take some leadership, church, and do something about it—because if you don't, the sin is going to spread. It's going to get worse. It's going to tear your

church apart. (Jesus lays out a process for this in Matthew 18:15–20; read there for more information on how to do this.)

In our world of iTunes, Oprah's Book Club, and Barnes & Noble, there are all kinds of voices vying for our attention. That's a good thing. But we have to be careful. We have to use discernment, because not everything that's out there is true. Some people try to use Scripture (out of context) to justify what they're teaching. Look for fruit. Are people coming to Christ as a result of this teaching? Any true work of God is going to have people who are repenting of their sin and coming to Christ. There are a lot of great teachers out there who, frankly, are just building a following for themselves, and there is no real fruit.

Finally, 1 Corinthians 11:31 says, "But if we judged ourselves, we would not come under judgment." Men, let me tell you, if you really want to blow your wife's mind, go to her and say, "You know what, babe? I have been doing some self-analysis, and I realized I have been dropping the ball on keeping the house straight and doing my part and carrying my weight. I apologize for that and want you to know I'm going to do my best from now on." Honestly, you're going to get judged on that either way, right? Either she's going to do the judging, or you're going to do the judging. It's a lot easier, wouldn't you agree, if we judge ourselves in some areas?

Those are a few examples of areas we should judge as Christians, so clearly the Bible doesn't say that we should never judge anything. So what was Jesus talking about when he said, "Do not judge"? The problem is that the church has been known to take judgment to the other extreme. I mean, we have become known as a very judgmental group of people. And when judgment gets out of whack, it's like an antibody that starts attacking the wrong things. It becomes an autoimmune disease in the church, the body of Christ. So here are some other things we just shouldn't judge.

Romans 14:1 says, "Accept him whose faith is weak, without passing judgment on disputable matters." There are always going to be things we can't agree on, aren't there? Back in Paul's day, it was, should you eat meat or not? Today it's, what style of music should you use in worship? Should you vote Democrat or Republican? We all have different points of view on those issues on which the Bible isn't black-and-white. If you take something that is a personal conviction and judge other people by it, you become an antibody that is attacking the wrong things.

Next, the Bible says:

My brothers, as believers in our glorious Lord Jesus Christ, don't show favoritism. Suppose a man comes into your meeting wearing a gold ring and fine clothes, and a poor man in shabby clothes also comes in. If you show special attention to the man wearing fine clothes and say, "Here's a good seat for you," but say to the poor man, "You stand there" or "Sit on the floor by my feet," have you not discriminated among yourselves and become judges with evil thoughts? (James 2:1–4)

We shouldn't judge based on outward appearance, but we do this, don't we? We judge people based on how they vote or what color their skin is, what kind of car they drive, what part of the city they live in. When we refuse to look beyond the outside of a person, we're missing the part of them that God wants us to see.

When we judge non-Christians, we do damage to the mission and the purpose God has for us. As 1 Corinthians 5:12 says, "What business is it of mine to judge those outside the church?" Jesus says that he "came to seek and to save the lost" (Luke 19:10). We can't expect non-Christians to act like Christians. It is God's love that leads us to repentance, not the judgment of Christians. When we judge non-Christians, we give up on them before God does. And when we judge people who aren't Christians, we forget where we came from. We attack the mission we're supposed to be on.

Finally, 1 Corinthians 4:5 says, "Therefore judge nothing before the appointed time; wait till the Lord comes. He will bring to light what is hidden in darkness and will expose the motives of men's hearts." The Bible says God will expose the motives of others. We can't do that.

Jesus tells us that it is possible to avoid a judgmental spirit. How? Forgive rather than condemn. Luke 6:37 says, "Do not condemn, and you will not be condemned. Forgive, and you will be forgiven." Are there people in your life who, every time their names come up, cause negative thoughts to jump into your brain? Forgive them. The scary thing about unforgiveness is that when you let it sit for a while, it turns into bitterness, and bitterness destroys you.

Be a giver instead of a taker. Luke 6:38 says, "Give, and it will be given to you." Moms seem to get this principle, don't they? They're always taking us to sporting events and staying home with us when we're sick and constantly giving of their resources, time, and talent. And they never complain about it,

NOTES

never are critical about it. Aren't you thankful for moms like that? The truth is, generosity naturally sets itself up against a critical spirit. When you're critical, you're automatically taking away. So we need to be givers rather than takers.

NOTES

Learn to be a learner, not a critic. In Luke 6:40, Jesus says, "A student is not above his teacher, but everyone who is fully trained will be like his teacher." Several years ago, I had the opportunity to join other pastors for lunch with Rick Warren, author of *The Purpose Driven Life*. Rick showed up to the restaurant with a big yellow legal pad. After he met everyone, he started firing off questions. You have to understand . . . this guy has a church of thirty thousand people. He has written multiple books on church leadership. But here he was, asking us, "How do you guys do church?" and taking pages and pages of notes. He's committed to being a lifelong learner. I want to be that way. It'll help me to avoid a critical spirit.

Finally, be a plank remover, not a speck inspector. Luke 6:41–42 says, "Why do you look at the speck of sawdust in your brother's eye and pay no attention to the plank in your own eye? How can you say to your brother, 'Brother, let me take the speck out of your eye,' when you yourself fail to see the plank in your own eye? You hypocrite, first take the plank out of your eye, and then you will see clearly to remove the speck from your brother's eye."

Think about a surgeon coming in to fix a speck in somebody's eye when he has a plank in his own eye. We'd stay far away from him, wouldn't we? We wouldn't want to have anything to do with him. Wouldn't you agree that most of us have enough issues under our own roof to deal with instead of focusing on other people's issues? We need to be plank removers instead of speck inspectors.

It's important that, as Christians, we learn to be discerning people, but we shouldn't cross over into judgment. The truth is, we're only hurting ourselves when we do that. We'll learn less, trust less, and doubt more. God calls us to be *believers*, so we should focus on believing what he tells us and leave the judging up to him.

[**READ**]

Carefully read through the following passage. Although this scripture is pretty well-known, don't let that color your reading. Look for something new, something you haven't seen before. What stands out to you? How does this enhance and add to the lesson in the last session?

"'Do not judge, and you will not be judged. Do not condemn, and you will not be condemned. Forgive, and you will be forgiven. Give, and it will be given to you. A good measure, pressed down, shaken together and running over, will be poured into your lap. For with the measure you use, it will be measured to you.'

"He also told them this parable: 'Can a blind man lead a blind man? Will they not both fall into a pit? A student is not above his teacher, but everyone who is fully trained will be like his teacher.

NOTES

"'Why do you look at the speck of sawdust in your brother's eye and pay no attention to the plank in your own eye? How can you say to your brother, "Brother, let me take the speck out of your eye," when you yourself fail to see the plank in your own eye? You hypocrite, first take the plank out of your eye, and then you will see clearly to remove the speck from your brother's eye'" (Luke 6:37–42).

1. Read verses 37–38. What two things does Jesus tell us we are not to do? What do these words mean? Why do these things have no place in the life of a follower of Jesus? See James 2:8–13.

2. Jesus doesn't just tell us not to do something. Again, he tells us to replace old attitudes with new ones. What two things should we do instead? How do these contrast with the things that we are not to do?

3. Luke 6:39–42 contains two examples regarding sight. What are they? What do the examples teach us about judgment? How do these tie together?

For further study, spend some time this week meditating on these two parables. Ask God to reveal how they tend to play out in your own life and how you can learn to be less judgmental.

[**REFLECT**]

1. How have you been challenged and/or encouraged so far in this study regarding grace, prayer, blessing, and reconciliation? How does what you've learned impact this discussion on passing judgment?

2. Why do we tend to want grace for ourselves and judgment for others?

3. Do you have a tendency to judge others? Think back over the last few days or weeks. Can you think of a time when you judged or condemned someone? For what did you judge the person?

4. Do you have anyone in your life to help you remove the planks and specks from your own eye? Who is it? How does this person help you do that?

5. How does it feel to point out others' specks? How does it feel to let go of your own planks?

6. If we are not to judge moral failure, what is our responsibility to our brothers and sisters in Christ? How can we help one another become more Christlike without being hypocritical or judgmental?

[ACTION STEPS]

⊃ Spend some time confessing the ways you have judged others recently. Remember, Jesus said, "With the measure you use, it will be measured to you" (Luke 6:38). Then spend time in celebration thanking God for his love and mercy. Ask God to help you show the same love and mercy to others.

⊃ With your small group, decide how you will treat one another. If you haven't already, create a small-group covenant, committing yourselves to one another, abounding with grace and avoiding judgment.

[**GROUP DISCUSSION**]

Welcome to session five of your small group study of Luke 6!

ICE BREAKER

> Have you ever been on the
> receiving end of someone else's
> judgment? How did it make
> you feel? How did it affect your
> relationship with that person?

Reflections from the Week

Depending on your group size, break into groups of two or three and share the following:

• Review your notes and observations from your personal study time. What have you learned from the readings? Are there any questions you would like to discuss with the group?

• What stood out to you in completing the spiritual gifts test in session four? Were you surprised by the results? How did the results confirm what you knew about yourself? How can you put your gifts to use? (If you didn't log on to www.eleventalents.com to complete the spiritual gifts test in session four, take some time to do that this week.)

• As a group, record everyone's top gift. Collectively, how can your group use these gifts to make a difference?

[WATCH DVD] Session 5

➲ *Discussion Questions*

1. What are some reasons we judge other people? Are these reasons built on the truth of God's Word? Why or why not?

2. Why is it so important to God that we don't compare ourselves to others?

3. What are some things we need to remember in order to keep us from judging others?

4. When does judgment benefit the community?

For Next Time

Ask God to multiply and use your group's spiritual gifts. Find opportunities to put your gifts to use—look for volunteer opportunities within your church and community. Select and schedule an outreach project and watch God use your group to impact your community.

Close in [PRAYER]

Father, thank you for loving us so much that you sent your Son to take on the form of humanity and to teach us and to model for us how we're to live our lives. Convict our hearts, God, that we would turn to you, repent of our sin, and turn the focus back inward. Show us how we can grow, how we can love our families better, and how we can model your love in a stronger way. In Jesus' name, amen.

[**YOUTH** **DISCUSSION**]

Welcome to your fifth session of discussion of Luke 6!

This Session's [BIG] Idea

Worry about the plank before the speck.

Memory Verse

"Why worry about a speck in your friend's eye when you have a log in your own?" (Luke 6:41 NLT).

[WATCH DVD] Session 5

➲ *Discussion Questions*

1. Why do you think God does not want us to judge others?

2. What is the difference between correcting and judging?

3. Why is it important to correct our own sin before we correct the sins of others?

Challenge

Take some time this week to look at your life. Is there an area of sin that you need to clean out?

[**FAMILY DISCUSSION**]

Message: Mind your own business.

[LIFEBOOK] Idea of the Week

Jesus teaches about working on ourselves first (Luke 6:37–42).

Summary

It's easy to see what others are doing wrong, isn't it? Jesus knew this, so he taught the people to be careful and worry about doing the right thing themselves *before* they looked at what others were doing.

[LIFELINE] The Main Point

Jesus wants me to let him work on my heart.

[LIFEVERSE] Memorize This!

"It's easy to see a smudge on your neighbor's face and be oblivious to the ugly sneer on your own" (Luke 6:41 MSG).

[LIFECHALLENGE]

Talk together as a family.

1. Why do you think it's easier to see the wrong that others do?

2. Do you think it's hard to mind your own business? In what ways do you think God will bless us if we do?

Action

⮕ Is there a fun way that your family can help one another remember not to criticize others? Put your brains together and see if you can come up with a family plan. Here's an idea: If someone gets caught saying something bad about someone else, he or she has to pay a quarter into the "family fun" jar or do an extra chore around the house. Can you come up with another one?

NOTES

Luke 6:43–49

FOUNDATIONS

The good man brings
good things out of the
good stored up in his
heart, and the evil man
brings evil things out
of the evil stored up in
his heart. For out of the
overflow of his heart
his mouth speaks.

—Luke 6:45

[PERSONAL DISCOVERY]

CONSIDER By Greg Surratt

Have you ever made an online purchase you were really excited about, only to have it delivered, unpack it, and find out it wasn't nearly as good as it looked online? Jesus addressed this issue when it comes to our hearts too. "A good tree can't produce bad fruit," he said. "And a bad tree can't produce good fruit" (Luke 6:43 NLT). If your package is that of a "good tree," your spirit needs to match it. So which are you—a good tree or a bad tree? How do you know for sure? It's all about knowing your foundation for living.

Wouldn't it be great if the world was full of people who were all "good trees"? We could live in paradise, right? Remember the song "Imagine"? As a part of John Lennon's vision for world peace and the brotherhood of men, he had this dream: we could be one, and there would be peace. But unfortunately, Lennon's plan for world peace won't happen because he didn't address the biggest problem in the world today—our evil hearts.

Now, I'm not waiting for the world to get horrible and Jesus to come rapture us out of the mess. That might happen, but I think that if we become like Jesus and we live his life, we can make the world a better place. It starts in our hearts and then grows and spreads to our families, our communities, our countries, and the world. Perhaps world peace would be possible if we would live as Jesus would have us to live.

Tim Keller, pastor at Redeemer Presbyterian Church in New York, says, "Christianity has rich resources that can make its followers agents for peace on earth. Christianity has within itself remarkable power to explain and expunge divisive tendencies within the human heart."[1] Because the biggest problem in the world today is an evil heart.

You may not think your heart is *evil*, exactly. Have you ever said or done anything that made you think, *Where did that come from?* Perhaps you did something you were ashamed of. Well, let me tell you where it came from. It came from your heart. Your heart is evil. Psalm 51:5 says, "For I was born a sinner—yes, from the moment my mother conceived me" (NLT).

We all want to do better. That's why we make New Year's resolutions. We try to eat less, drink less, cuss less, spend less . . . but out of our sinful nature, a bad heart, comes a sinful life. Does Romans 3:23 say, "For most people have sinned"? No, it says, "For *all* have sinned and fall short of the glory of God" (emphasis added).

You've been lied to. You've been told by talk shows, books, and magazines that you're inherently good, and you're born morally neutral, and you just need to do good things. It's not true. The truth is, you are a bad person and you can only do bad things because you

have a heart problem, an evil heart. That is the problem in the world today.

So what do we do about our evil hearts? The solution to an evil heart is a heart transplant. The Bible says our problem is so bad we don't just need a bypass; we need a transplant. We need a whole new heart. In Ezekiel 11, God is dealing with the people of Israel, because they wander off all the time. They're constantly doing stuff that ticks God off and hurts people. In Ezekiel 11, God says there's coming a day when: "I will give them an undivided heart and put a new spirit in them; I will remove from them their heart of stone and give them a heart of flesh" (v. 19).

Religion doesn't get you anywhere. Just trying to do, do, do. Trying to take that old heart and make it better, better, better, but you keep on sinning. There's only one way to fix it: Jesus. God says he will accept and acquit us—declare us not guilty—if we trust Jesus Christ to take away our sins. We all can be saved in this same way: by coming to Christ, no matter who we are or what we've done. That's the beginning of the process. It's called being born again.

Once this change happens in our lives, we start to build that foundation that will never crumble. It's Jesus as the solid underpinning of our souls. Even after we've come to Jesus and given him our sinful selves, though, we still make mistakes. We still screw up. So how do we know that we've had a heart transplant?

Scripture gives us a few ways to identify that our foundation is Jesus. These are ways we can clearly see that the packaging of "Christ-follower" matches the content of our lives: Your heart has a hunger for God. You desire to love people. You're quick to repent. There is evidence of change in your actions and habits.

Someday God will separate the good hearts from the evil hearts, the saints from the sinners. And they're going to different places. You want to be in the right line. James 1:22 (NLT) says, "Don't just listen to God's word. You must do what it says. Otherwise, you are only fooling yourselves." He says you're just fooling yourself because the evidence of a successful heart transplant is a changed life, a heart for God, a love for people.

Here's the foundation on which you need to build your life: God is good, and his mercy endures forever.

[**READ**]

Carefully read the following passage. This is still part of Jesus'
sermon to his disciples that began in Luke 6:20. What stands out to
you? At first glance, what are some of the characteristics of Christ-
followers found here?

*"'No good tree bears bad fruit, nor does a bad tree bear good fruit. Each tree
is recognized by its own fruit. People do not pick figs from thornbushes, or
grapes from briers. The good man brings good things out of the good stored
up in his heart, and the evil man brings evil things out of the evil stored up
in his heart. For out of the overflow of his heart his mouth speaks.*

*"'Why do you call me, "Lord, Lord," and do not do what I say? I will
show you what he is like who comes to me and hears my words and puts
them into practice. He is like a man building a house, who dug down deep
and laid the foundation on rock. When a flood came, the torrent struck that*

house but could not shake it, because it was well built. But the one who hears my words and does not put them into practice is like a man who built a house on the ground without a foundation. The moment the torrent struck that house, it collapsed and its destruction was complete'" (Luke 6:43–49).

1. The image of a tree and its fruit is often used throughout Scripture to explain spiritual truths. According to Jesus, what can this image teach us about the heart of a person?

2. In verses 46–49, Jesus gives us a second analogy representing the relationship between a person's heart and his or her outward behavior. Read carefully through this section. Make a list of the various images. What do you think they represent? For example, what does the flood stand for? The rock?

3. Jesus' sermon throughout Luke 6 continually reinforces one idea: It is not enough for a follower of Christ to just do certain things or act a certain way. He or she must be a certain type of person—one who has submitted everything to the Lord. This requires a complete overhaul from the inside out. How do the examples in this session's passage support this idea?

CHRIST-FOLLOWER

C. S. Lewis once wrote:

> To trust Him means, of course, trying to do all that He says.
> There would be no sense in saying you trusted a person if
> you would not take his advice. Thus if you have really handed
> yourself over to Him, it must follow that you are trying to obey
> Him. But trying in a new way, a less worried way. Not doing
> these things in order to be saved, but because He has begun
> to save you already. Not hoping to get to Heaven as a reward
> for your actions, but inevitably wanting to act in a certain way
> because a first faint gleam of Heaven is already inside you.[2]

Meditate on this quote, concentrating on what it means to live a
life completely in obedience to the Lord. Rejoice in what God has
done in your life and the world, and what he is continuing to do.

For further study, examine what Scripture says about "fruit" in our lives. Concordances and topical Bibles are useful tools for this type of study. Don't have one? Check out www.biblegateway.com or www.lifeway.com/Bible.

[**REFLECT**]

1. Think about the "fruit" in your own life. Is this fruit indicative of a good or bad tree? In other words, what do your words and actions say about the condition of your heart?

2. How do you filter what you hear so that you know what should or should not become a part of who you are and how you act?

3. Read John 15:1–11. How are we able to bear fruit? Why is our fruit important to our witness in the world? (See verse 8.)

4. Jesus compares building on a weak foundation to building on a firm foundation. Have you experienced construction problems from cutting corners, not preparing properly, or not following the blueprints? What was the result?

5. When trouble and hard times come your way, do you tend to stand strong or fall apart? Why do you think this is?

6. How can you encourage one another to be better doers of the Word and not just hearers?

7. Reread Luke 6:46. How would you answer Jesus' question?

[ACTION STEPS]

➲ What do you know God wants you to stop doing, but you have not yet acted on it? Confess this area to him and stop immediately. For support, discuss this with your accountability partner, or put it on paper (your Spiritual Growth Plan from session two).

➲ What do you know God wants you to start doing, but you have not yet acted on it? Confess this area to him and start immediately. For support, discuss this with your accountability partner, or put it on paper.

➲ Think of two things you can do to make it clear to yourself and the world around you that your foundation is Christ alone. Write them here and look back on them daily this week.

1.

2.

➲ This week, memorize John 15:5.

[**GROUP DISCUSSION**]

Welcome to your final session of small group study of Luke 6!

BREAKER

> If you were to grade yourself on how well you put God's Word into practice this past week, what grade would you give yourself?

Reflections from the Week

Depending on your group size, break into groups of two or three and share the following:

• Review your notes and observations from the personal study time. What have you learned from the readings? Are there any questions you would like to discuss with the group?

• Spend some time discussing your experiences over the last six sessions. How do you think you have grown?

• As a group, discuss ways in which you can continue to challenge one another to grow and to be doers of the Word, not just hearers of the Word.

[WATCH DVD] SESSION 6

➲ *Discussion Questions*

1. What are the two things Jesus teaches us in Luke 6:46–49 we need to do?

2. What are some challenges to putting Jesus' words into practice?

CHRIST-
FOLLOWER

3. Are you building on your spiritual foundation daily? If so, in what ways?

4. Are there any weak areas you can identify? What are some practical ways you can build on your foundation this week?

For Next Time

Your spiritual growth does not stop at the end of this study. It is ongoing! Encourage one another to meet with accountability partners and to identify ways to utilize your spiritual gifts, and periodically assess your spiritual growth as a group.

Close in [PRAYER]

Spend time as a group praying out loud about what God has taught you over the last six sessions.

[**YOUTH DISCUSSION**]

Welcome to your final session of discussion of Luke 6!

THIS SESSION'S [BIG] IDEA

We are known by the type of "fruit" (or actions) we produce.

Memory Verse

"A good person produces good things from the treasury of a good heart, and an evil person produces evil things from the treasury of an evil heart. What you say flows from what is in your heart" (Luke 6:45 NLT).

 [WATCH DVD] **SESSION 6**

➲ *Discussion Questions*

1. How do we control what goes into our hearts?

2. What does it mean to produce good fruit?

3. What kind of fruit do you think you produce?

Challenge

Reflect upon whether you think your friends view you as a Christian. What can you do this week to make your faith more obvious?

[**FAMILY DISCUSSION**]

Message: It's what's in your heart that counts.

[LIFEBOOK] **Idea of the Week**

Jesus teaches the importance of having the right heart and doing the right things (Luke 6:43–49).

Summary

Jesus uses two stories to show us that we need to make sure we've given our hearts completely over to him, because what's in our hearts will show to others. If we have good in our hearts, then we will be able to do good things for God.

[LIFELINE] **The Main Point**

What's inside our hearts shows on the outside.

[LIFEVERSE] **Memorize This!**

"A good person produces good things from the treasury of a good heart" (Luke 6:45 NLT).

[LIFECHALLENGE]

Talk together as a family.

1. Jesus used the example of a tree being recognized by its fruit. Do other people know you are a Christian? How do they know?

2. Do you think it's enough to just tell people about God, or do you think God wants us to show others about his love through the things we do? How can we do this?

Action

➲ What things can your family do together to show others that your family serves the Lord? Make a list of ideas and then do them!

NOTES

[NOTES]

Session One: Calm

1. Nan Fink, *Stranger in the Midst: A Memoir of Spiritual Discovery* (New York: Basic Books, 1997), 95–96.

Session Two: Choices

1. Richard Foster, *Prayer: Finding the Heart's True Home* (New York: HarperOne, 1992), 13–14.

Session Three: Blessings

1. Dallas Willard, *The Divine Conspiracy: Rediscovering Our Hidden Life in God* (New York: HarperOne, 1998), 106.

Session Four: Love

1. Edward W. Goodrick and John R. Kohlrenberger III, *The Strongest NIV Exhaustive Concordance* (Grand Rapids: Zondervan, 2004), s.v. "reward."

2. G. B. Caird, in *Augsburg Sermons 3, Gospel Series C* (Minneapolis: Augsburg Books, 1994), 42.

Session Six: Foundations

1. Timothy Keller, *The Reason for God: Belief in an Age of Skepticism* (New York: Penguin, 2008), 18.

2. C. S. Lewis, *Mere Christianity* (New York: HarperCollins, 2001), 147–48.

[**ABOUT THE AUTHORS**]

Seacoast Church

Seacoast Church is one of the fastest-growing and most influential churches in the Southeast, with weekend attendance of nearly 11,000 spread over thirteen campuses in three states (North Carolina, South Carolina, Georgia) and on the Internet.

Greg Surratt

Greg is a founding pastor of Seacoast Church and also a founding board member of the Association of Related Churches (ARC), a church-planting network that has given birth to 135 churches in the last nine years.

Josh Surratt

Josh came on staff at Seacoast in 2001 working in student ministries. Since then, Josh has served as the connect pastor and provided leadership for life groups throughout the transition from a single campus to multiple campuses. In his current role as campus pastor, he is excited about the opportunity to connect people in our community to the love of Christ.

Geoff Surratt

Geoff is the pastor of ministries at Seacoast Church. Geoff has overseen Seacoast's expansion from one to thirteen locations across three states and from three thousand to more than ten thousand weekend attendees. He works with other churches across the country in strategic planning and staff development and has also helped train leaders in Europe, Asia, and Africa. He has written the following books: *Ten Stupid Things That Keep Churches from Growing, The Multisite Church Revolution,* and *A Multisite Church Roadtrip.*